Send A Refreshing

POETIC PRAYERS OF AN INTERCESSOR

Desiree McCray

Send a Refreshing: Poetic Prayers of an Intercessor

Copyright © 2021 by Desiree McCray

All rights reserved. No part of this publication may be reproduced in any form or by any means, electronic, mechanical, photocopying, recording, or otherwise, without the prior written permission of the author and copyright owner, except where permitted by law.

This book is sold subject to the condition that it shall not, by way of trade or otherwise, be lent, resold, hired out, or otherwise circulated without the publisher's prior consent. Under no circumstances may any part of this book be photocopied for resale.

ISBN:979-8-9859491-1-7

Editing by Desiree McCray Printed and Bound in the USA First Printing 2022

This book is dedicated to Holy Spirit
Who leads me along paths of righteousness

TABLE OF CONTENT

Introduction 1
What is prayer? 6
—Prayer for Every day— 11
—Prayer for the Weary—....................................... 13
—Prayer of Deliverance— 15
—Prayer of Offering—.. 17
—Prayer of Confession For Election Day 2020—.. 18
—Prayer for Being in the Word—.......................... 20
—Prayer before preaching—................................. 21
—A Prayer for God's Peace— 23
—Prayers of the People— 26
—Prayer for Dependence on God— 31
—Prayer for the Black Woman—.......................... 33
—Prayer for the Black Man— 35
—Prayer for Witness— 37
—Prayer for Youth—.. 39
—Bedtime Prayer—.. 41

—A Prayer for Loss of Loved Ones— 43

—A Prayer for Rejects— 45

—A Prayer for Transformation—. 47

—A Prayer for Transition— 49

—A Prayer for Courage— 51

—Prayer for Doubt— 53

—Prayer for Revival— 55

—A Prayer for Purification— 57

—Prayer for Healing— 59

—A Prayer for Faith— 61

About The Author 63

Books By This Author 64

Forthcoming books 65

INTRODUCTION

The devil comes to steal, kill & destroy, but Jesus came so we might have life more abundantly. Life is what I have learned to cling to. All aspects of life. The good, the bad, the ebb and flow, the dark and light, the natural and the supernatural, the ordinary and the extraordinary. "Every day above ground is a good day," someone once said.

Prayer as a start to my morning helps me live more fully by starting my day with inner quiet, stillness, and deep gratitude. I realize prayer has changed my life. After all, the life I'm enjoying now is the result of not only my prayers but the prayers of my ancestors. My fulfilled prayers were some of their wildest dreams.

Going to college and finishing two-degree programs, publishing my first book *Hope Among Other Foods*, opening my art business, walking in my calling as a pastor, and becoming an award-winning preacher who preaches across the world all live on as a result of prayer. These are all things I prayed for that God's word manifested in my life. I am manifesting blessings as the result of asking God and believing I would receive what God has for me.

When I was happy, I prayed.

When I was desperate, I prayed.

When I felt alone, I prayed.

When I felt anxious, I prayed.

When I felt worried, I prayed.

When I felt depressed, I prayed.

When I felt thankful, I prayed because as a kid I learned that God could handle all of me because he made all of me. I learned as a child that God wanted me to keep talking to him, and keep bowing before him even when I felt ashamed, lost, or broken. My relationship with God taught me that God always desires a relationship with me no matter what mood or emotion I might be feeling.

Knowing that God desires me in every mental and emotional state makes intimacy with God so much easier. I know God will listen to me and doesn't see

Introduction

my problems as petty because God cares about the things that trouble me. However, my big problems do not compare to the Bigness of my Big God. We serve a big God who's bigger than our troubles and brokenness.

God's bigness is the key mindset approach I had when writing these very personal yet public prayers. Having community with God requires us to understand we must be vulnerable with God. We must bring our whole selves, identities, and experiences to our experience of prayer. If we aren't vulnerable with God, we do ourselves a disservice by hiding from the same One that knows and created our innermost being. There's nothing God does not know about us. God knows all so it makes no sense to hide our truth from God.

I hope these prayers will remind you of who God is, and what God is capable of, and that refreshing comes in the small whisper of God. I hope this short book of prayers brings you healing for your soul. I didn't write these prayers for anyone, in particular, I simply wrote the prayers in a post-Trump, pandemic heavily-laden world. I wrote what I knew I needed. And as I prayed I saw God transform not only the world around me but me in the world.

Desiree McCray

As I prayed I felt as if I was under an open heaven as if God was hearing and responding. I felt like my spirit was edified and built up. I felt as if I was being stirred from the inside out and I knew I had to release these prayers that are deposited from heaven. I knew that many would be blessed by my obedience in publishing this refreshment in book form. Thank you for allowing God to bless you by supporting me.

May these words manifest a life lived well for you.

May you experience soul-refreshing.

May you find God again.

May you tremble in awe of the results of these prayers.

May you be blessed beyond belief.

May you retreat from constant busyness and stress to find God while God can still be found.

May God send a fresh wind and fresh anointing in your direction as you digest God's word.

May God send a refreshing to you starting now!

Let your prayers be bridges over troubled and troubling waters.

> "A day without prayer is a day without blessing, and a life without prayer is a life without power."
>
> - Edwin Harvey

WHAT IS PRAYER?

Most simply prayer is a dialogue—a conversation with the God of the Universe. Dialogue implies that two or more people are in conversation. So, prayer is not a monologue with one person speaking; therefore, we ought to wait for a response from the Lord. During prayer, we are not talking *at* God. We are talking *to* God and what a privilege it is to be able to convene with God who holds the whole world in Her hands.

We believe that we are speaking to a God who hears us. God receives our prayers with gladness. The Bible tells us in James 5:16 "The prayers of a righteous man are potent and fruitful." As the ancestors vocalize, "prayer changes things." During alter call one Sunday morning at The Congregational Church of Park Manor in Chicago, Illinois, Reverend Dr. Terrill Murff declared "little prayer, little power; many prayers, much power."

What is prayer?

Prayer remains a powerful tool, a weapon to clarify life's confusion and confront life's conditions. Too often prayer becomes used as a last resort rather than a first step. I hope this book actives your prayer life as proactive rather than simply reactive. Prayer is our first defense against despair and hopelessness faced in this world. Prayer reminds us that victory is ours in Christ.

Sometimes, we do not know how or for what we ought to pray. During these times, prayer often involves meditating on the word of God. The Bible tells us that Jesus would often slip away to the wilderness to pray (*Luke 5:16*). Just as Jesus slipped away, we must slip away to be with God. Slip away from our everyday tasks. Slip away from our busyness. In an age of constant connection, we must disconnect to reconnect to the Creator.

Prayer can be aloud or held in our hearts. Prayer can be corporate or personal. No matter the setting, our minds should stay focused on the hope of our salvation while we pray. As my ancestor sang, "Woke up this morning with my mind stayed on Jesus", the ancestors knew that prayer is not just words, but a posture. A posture of staying our minds on Jesus.

Desiree McCray

When we pray, we approach the throne of grace with the utmost humility because God is greater than us. God is holy and if we are honest, not one can stand before the Lord, for all have fallen short of the glory of God (Romans 3:23). For those who have faith and are saved by grace, we pray believing that God knows what we pray for before we even ask (Matthew 6:8).

We (intercessors) pray when we exhaust ourselves in labor. We pray when we can't utter words. We pray to the silence even. We pray the prayer from the depths of our souls and our hearts can only move to become more softened as we derelict. So we learn to lament in new ways.

We receive a new mantle of praise, a new tongue of thanksgiving to pray new specific strategies. Yes, God will refresh our prayer life if we learn to adapt to our circumstances. If we look at how prayer has brought us, we know Kairos (God's Time) is perfect. We must pray at the proper time and learn to express new forms and fashions of prayer in a new season.

When I was taught to pray in my Junior Deacon Ordination in 2012, I learned the "ACTS" method of prayer from Reverend Rhoda Barnes. This formula remains easy to remember and has served as a resource for me when I needed to "get back to basics."

Adoration

Example:

- "Lord, we love you"
- "Heavenly Father, you are great and greatly to be praised"

1. Tell God how good God is
2. Worship God

Confession

Example:

- "I admit I have not always done what was right"
- "We confess that we have sinned in thought, word, and Deed"

1. Confess your sins and ask for forgiveness
2. Be vulnerable with God about where you went wrong

Desiree McCray

Thanksgiving

Example:

- "Lord, we thank you"
- "Thank you for protecting me, Jesus"

1. Give God thanks
2. Show gratitude for all that God has done

Supplication

Example:

- "Lord, bless my family"
- "Lord, touch my mind and help me to be more like you"

1. Make your requests known to our Mother in Heaven
2. Tell the Lord what you need

—PRAYER FOR EVERY DAY—

Dear Heavenly Father,

Lord, thank You for my mind. May the Creator grant me more power in my mind. May everything with my health be well. May I receive divine direction toward my purpose and destiny. May God build my confidence. May God prune me for the better. May God purify my desires. May God refine me in the fire. As I go through this transformational process, May God transform my heart, mind, and soul and conform them to the image of Jesus Christ. May my eyes be opened to God's spirit and to see the face of God in everyone I meet. May I not strive to please people but to please You with my life. May God's will be done in my life. May my life be an example of God's grace, holiness, and favor. May I walk in the way of love, in abundant life, in victory & prosperity. Thank You, Lord, for who You are. Thank You for all that You have done, will do, and are doing right now for me. I glorify Your name and lift You. May my life glorify You as I serve You.

IN JESUS NAME. Amen

—PRAYER FOR THE WEARY—

Lover of My Soul,

Thank You for fighting my battles when I feel weak. Thank You for strengthening me when I feel desperate and weary in my walk. Help me to lean on You and to rely on You more when life becomes draining and unpredictable. Help me when I feel worn and tired of fighting. Fortify me that I may be steadfast when I feel ready to give up. Allow me to rest when I feel like I can't go on. Reassure me that Your path before me is divinely guided. Even when the enemy seems busy, remind me that You're busy guiding me and blessing me with new breath each day. You just won't let me go. Thank You for fighting for me today. Fill me with the power of the Holy Spirit and grant me joy because the Joy of the Lord is my strength. When life is drying, when discouragement & despair abounds, may the refreshing, living waters refill me to overflow (John 7:38). May You give me a word to encourage me, a smile to uplift me, a note to remind me, a prayer to cover someone else. For I know I am not alone in this battle. Lord, Your word says, if God is for me, who can be against me? (Romans 8:31) May I know that You have sent others to hold up my battle-weary arms and that You are with us when we pray.

In Jesus' Name. Amen.

—PRAYER OF DELIVERANCE—

Mighty Deliverer,

El Shaddai (Lord God Almighty) You have all power in Your hands. Elohim, I love You and thank You for covering me in the Blood of Jesus. Hide me in your pavilion for You are my refuge. Your word says that greater is the one who is in me than the one who is in the world (1 John 4:4) Right now, I submit myself under Your authority, God. I resist the devil and he will flee (James 4:7). I repent for my sins that have divided me from You. Keep me from all temptation. Protect me from all evil. Deliver me from the enemy's hands. For I seek You and You answer me. You deliver me from all my fears (Psalm 34:4). Deliver me from all my troubles. You are my rock and the horn of my salvation (Psalm 18:2). You are my rock on whom I can rely. Deliver me from every bodily affliction. Deliver me from strongholds and break every yoke trying to hinder me in Jesus' Name. I cancel every demonic disruption of my life in the name of Jesus. I declare the work of the devil destroyed. El Shaddai, You have the final authority and power over every force of darkness in the spiritual realm. In the name of Jesus Christ and by the power of the blood and the Holy Spirit, I declare myself: delivered, placed, and positioned in Your right hand. Your word says "whatsoever is bound on earth is bound in heaven; what is loosed on earth, is loosed in heaven." (Matt. 16: 19). I bind satan, every evil spirit, powers, and forces of darkness in Jesus' Name. I bind any demonic transfer sent against me in the name of Jesus. I invoke the Holy Spirit, the Advocate, and angelic messengers and divine helpers in my life now. Cleanse me of every area of my life where the accuser has gained access to me. In the name of Jesus, I break and bind every curse, spell, hex, all acts of witchcraft, and demonic interference rising against me and passed down through my bloodline. I renounce and ask for Your forgiveness for any and every demonic covenant made in the spiritual realm in Jesus' Name. I divorce myself from all covenants and drench them in the blood of Jesus. Thanks be to God who gives me victory through the Lord Jesus Christ of Nazareth. In Jesus' Name Amen.

—PRAYER OF OFFERING—

Precious Lord, Giver of every good and perfect gift,

    We love You and We thank You for the gifts and the givers. This day You remind us of the word that says "Give, and it will be given to you. A good measure, pressed down, shaken together, and running over, will be poured into your lap. For with the measure you use, it will be measured to you."

    Lord, in our giving may we make room for more of You. We offer back just a portion of all that You have given us. We ask that You bless and multiply these gifts. Consecrate them for the building of Your kingdom here on earth as it is in heaven.

    We pray all these things with thanksgiving according to the goodness of Christ Our Lord. Amen.

—PRAYER OF CONFESSION FOR ELECTION DAY 2020—

Merciful and Gracious God,

We call on You to confess that we have sinned against You in thought, word, and deed. We have not loved You with all our hearts; we have not loved our neighbors as ourselves. For far too long, we have been numb; we have ignored the suffering in the world. At different times, we have been uncomfortable, ungrateful, unaffected, unwilling, uninformed, unresolved, or unable to find our way.

Lord, we need You and we need Your forgiveness. Please help us to lean on You. Help us to use our voices to make an impact in this upcoming election. Remind us that our voices and our votes count. Encourage our hearts to live our lives for You to the best of our ability. Have mercy upon us. Grant

— **Prayer of Confession For Election Day 2020—**

us freedom from any guilt or shame that keeps us from serving You. Restore us, renew us, reconstruct us, and reignite us according to Your goodness.

In Jesus' Name. Amen

—PRAYER FOR BEING IN THE WORD—

Heavenly Father and Mother,

We come to You thanking You for Your holy and true word. We pray that Your word would convict and correct us. We pray that Your word would reveal knowledge, wisdom, and even divine mystery. Please open our eyes with clarity while we study Your precious word.

May we not stray from the path Your word instructs. May You give us discernment as we apply Your word to our hearts. Renew us as we chew on and digest the goodness of Your word. Thank You for the words that encourage us, strengthen us, and lift us. Thank You for the words that chip away at us like a hammer (Jeremiah 23:29). May Your word continue to shape our hearts and minds. Bless our time in the word and fill us up with seeds of goodness that we pray will produce much fruit.

In Jesus' Name. Amen.

—PRAYER BEFORE PREACHING—

Loving and Gracious God,

I thank You for this word from on high. I pray Lord that You would purify me right now. Have Your way O God. Not my will but thine. I pray that the words of my mouth and the meditations of my heart would be acceptable to thee (Psalm 19:14).

Speak through me. Hide me behind the cross of Calvary so that the people would not see me or hear me. Instead, Lord, I pray they would see and hear You. I pray that this word is in the proper time and season for Your people. As I decrease, I ask that You increase.

Desiree McCray

Let your presence, power, and peace rest upon me now. I am a vessel and through You, I move and have my being. I pray with thanksgiving, giving You all the glory, honor, and praise. In Jesus's Matchless, Mighty, and Exalted Name I pray. Amen.

—A PRAYER FOR GOD'S PEACE—

Jehovah Shalom (The Lord Is Peace)

We know that the peace You give is not of this world. May we recognize the deep reward of being with You—a life of peace that surpasses all understanding. You are not the author of confusion but of peace (1 Corinthians 14: 33). May we trust and obey. Prepare us for greater in you. Lord, make us instruments of Your peace.

We pray for peace to fill our dwellings, our hearts, our country, and our world. Help us to be peacemakers and to seek to be peaceful in everything we do. When the storms of life are raging may Your words "Peace, be still" calm any storm.

Make us lie down in green pastures. Allow us to rest beside the still waters that You promised to provide (Psalm 23:2). Thank You for the resurrection of Your son Jesus Christ who declared peace no matter our circumstances, power over death and disease, and life more abundant. We trust in You.

In Jesus' Name. Amen.

> Please join me in this responsive litany by saying "Lord in your mercy, hear our prayer" when prompted.

—PRAYERS OF THE PEOPLE—

El Olam (The Everlasting God)

    We pray

    For the spirit of the living God to fall afresh on us.

    For peace to be our portion

    For faith to combat our frustrations For trust when we remain uncertain

    For vision when we can't see You working Open our eyes O God

    that we may seek You

    Let us pray to the Lord.

    Lord, in Your mercy, hear our prayer.

    [SILENCE]

    For the harvest that we reap

— Prayers of the People—

May we sow and water the seeds You've given us May our seed bear fruit in due season

May the fruit of our labor be a reminder:

O Taste and see that the Lord is Good

Let us pray to the Lord.

Lord, in Your mercy, hear our prayer.

[SILENCE]

For those lost and forgotten

For those oppressed by racist systems of injustice

For those facing terror, captivity, social isolation, and persecution

For those who hunger and thirst for righteousness that they may be filled

Let us pray to the Lord

Lord, in Your mercy, hear our prayer.

[SILENCE]

For those in our midst struggling with mental illness, health conditions, cancer, body aches

For those with chronic pain seeking healing

That in Your presence, O God,

We are made alive, renewed, and never the same

Let us pray to the Lord

Lord, in Your mercy, hear our prayer.

[SILENCE]

For us to go back to the moment when and where we first said yes And first received You

For us to remember that You can do more than we could ever ask for or imagine

For us who feel small or insignificant that we may find our purpose in You

And shine our light for Your glory

Let us pray to the Lord

Lord, in Your mercy, hear our prayer.

[SILENCE]

For all who have died in the hope of the resurrection, For all the departed, that they may rest eternally with You

For those facing violence abroad and domestically

— Prayers of the People —

For those hospitalized,

For the widowed and orphans for the sick and the suffering,

For the poor and the needy

Let us pray to the Lord

Lord, in Your mercy, hear our prayer.

[SILENCE]

For every church open in Jesus's name

For protection from all hurt, harm, and danger

That You may hide us in Your pavilion in the time of trouble

That we may recognize the angels around us to guide us in Your ways, O God

Let us pray to the Lord

Lord, in Your mercy, hear our prayer.

[SILENCE]

For reassurance that we are known and loved by You

Desiree McCray

For each of us is fearfully and wonderfully made in Your image

That we may become more like You

That You may grant us amazing grace as we journey with You in discipleship

Let us pray to the Lord

Lord, in Your mercy, hear our prayer.

In Jesus' Name. Amen.

—PRAYER FOR DEPENDENCE ON GOD—

Jehovah Tsidkenu (The Lord Our Righteousness)

There is nothing too hard for You. I need You every hour. Help me to write the vision and make it plain (Habakkuk 2:2). I empty myself before You so that You can fill me. I know that public prosperity does not prevent me from private pain. Yet I will not lose hope.

For You are the God who rescues me from all my fears. I want to know You more intimately. Put Your word in me and write it on my heart. May Your word show up in dark times. As I seek the word, may I also leak the word so that others may hear a word from You.

You are my refuge and my strength, an ever-present help in trouble. Because You are with me, I

Desiree McCray

cannot fall. Thank You for helping me when others forgot me. Give me the courage to depend on You for all my needs.

    I know that sometimes you allow me to go through situations just to show me how to trust you. You are showing me that grace abounds and that your grace is more than enough. Thank you.

    In Jesus' Name. Amen.

—PRAYER FOR THE BLACK WOMAN—

Light of the World,

When You formed the world in all its wonder You said, "it is beautiful." When you made the black woman You said "it is *very* beautiful." You gave black women such skin that their glow would glorify You—that You might identify her as Your very own.

You gave black women coils and curls that tell a story of defiance. You gifted black women bright eyes that prove them desirous to look upon all creation.

A nose ripened by the scents of sweet songs sung to You in praise.

You gave her Lips which denote a desire to be both heard and understood.

A cross, a symbol of the only one I fear—God who shall never forsake me.

O God, I bring to you the rage of black women being unprotected, underestimated, underrepresented, and undervalued in our society. I bring You joy in the black women being intelligent, resourceful, nurturing, and creative. I bring You exhaustion in seeing another shooting, another case of police brutality. I bring You pain of erasure through killings, domestic violence, sex trafficking, & sexual violence. We yell "SAY HER NAME" for our sisters who have fallen.

I call on you to bridge the gaps that leave black women at the margins and the intersections of race, gender, and class. We lay it all down at your altar. I declare that black women are no longer slaves but will all be free. I thank You that I am free from every bond that seeks to limit, chain, and oppress black women physically, spiritually, mentally, emotionally, and politically.

Black women do not live on anyone else's terms, but they seek to live for you. When haters arise to snuff out the inner light help black women to shine even brighter. And help us to remember that God gave his life for us. Thank you, Jesus. Help me to keep my eyes on You.

In Jesus' Name. Amen.

—PRAYER FOR THE BLACK MAN—

Alpha and Omega,

When You created the black man,

You smiled at the beauty that rests upon his shoulders.

You laughed at the light in his eyes that looks in wonder at all You have made.

You reveled in the soul possessed by his brown belly.

God thank You for creating the black man in all his splendor. We pray that You would cover him.

We ask that You lead him in paths of righteousness.

Lead him in Your ways of truth, love, and faithfulness.

Give him compassion where life has hardened him.

Give him faith where fear has stifled him.

Give him joy where life has burdened him.

Provide kind words and deeds where life has hated and halted his shine.

Provide words of encouragement when life has silenced him. Remind him that he does not have to be strong all the time, but in Your presence in his weakness, You are made strong. Raise the black man as a leader for the loss, protector of the vulnerable, and provider for those in need.

I pray Lord that You would protect him

from all hurt, harm, and dangers seen and unseen. Protect him as he resists the carceral state

which seeks his imprisonment, defeat, and demise.

May the black man walk in victory and in the knowledge of his capacity to captivate people with his gifts and abilities.

May he be empowered to walk fully in his call to be a co-creator in a life shaped by You.

In Jesus' Name. Amen.

—PRAYER FOR WITNESS—

El Roi (The God Who Sees Me),

In the Name of Jesus, I thank You that Your eye is on the sparrow. If You take care of the birds of the air, how much more will You take care of me? I have confidence that You are watching over me. You are the director of this movie called Life. You know my ending before my beginning. Even when I can't see, I know You see all and know all. You know me better than I know myself. I pray that You would strengthen my witness and bless my testimony before You in heaven. Help me to testify to others about Your goodness. Make me a bold witness for You. Give me a greater testimony to make known the great things You have done for me. I will not die, but I shall live and proclaim the works of the Lord (Psalm 118:17). I decree and declare that You are El Roi, the God who sees me. Help me to know that You see me even in moments when I feel invisible. Thank You for seeing

Desiree McCray

me and chasing after me all the days of my life. Help me to keep my eyes stayed on You. Give me Your eyes to see the way You do. In Jesus' Name. Amen.

—PRAYER FOR YOUTH—

Lord, I thank You for all your children and little ones. I pray for the youth to possess a spirit of humility. Grant them the fear of the Lord, purity of heart, wisdom that comes only from You. Make them a servant humble and meek. Strengthen those who are weak. Help them to obey their parents diligently. Help them to learn Your laws and keep Your commandments. Give them an open heart to receive Your love and to show compassion to their peers. As they grow in You, may their faith blossom. I plead the blood of Jesus over the youth in my life and ask that You cover them with Your feathers (Psalm 91:4). I pray they would display Christ-like behavior even when no one is watching. Give them ears to listen and a spirit surrendered to You. Help them to be confident in who You made them to be, for they are fearfully and wonderfully made (Psalm 139:14). May they fearlessly rely on You and submit to Your will. Heal them and

Desiree McCray

help them in every area. Grow in them the gifts of the Holy Spirit and the fruit of the Holy Spirit. Touch their minds that they may think of whatever is right, pure, noble, lovely, and admirable (Philippians 4:8). Keep them from all evil and preserve them as they grow healthy and grow in discipleship.

    I ask this in Jesus' name. Amen.

—BEDTIME PRAYER—

Jehovah Raah (The Lord is my Shepherd),

Thank You for blessing me throughout the day. Help me to sleep. Keep me from tossing and turning as I enter into sweet rest in the palm of Your hand. I'm thankful that I serve a God who neither sleeps nor slumbers. Thank You for Your constant presence with me now. Slow down my mind. Ease my anxieties and calm my worries. Comfort me as You lay me down to sleep. You are Jehovah Raah, The Lord is my shepherd. So I ask tonight that You lead me beside still waters that are ever flowing. Give me peace like a river. As I sleep give me dreams of You. Keep me safe in this hour of darkness. Send angels for each corner of the bed. May they watch and pray for me as I enter into sweet rest. Into Your hands, I commend myself: body, mind, and soul. I thank and praise You in advance for the wonderful rest I receive. I pray that I will awake refreshed and restored. May I awake stronger to endure tomorrow's challenges and be more grateful for tomorrow's joy to come in the morning light.

In Jesus' Name. Amen.

—A PRAYER FOR LOSS OF LOVED ONES—

Wonderful Counselor,

You are the Great Comforter. You are grieved by the loss of loved ones just as we are. Your only son died tragically and violently. I confess feelings of sadness, anger, hurt, regret, and/or confusion by the tragic loss I am facing. Sometimes I struggle to continue living now knowing that they have transitioned into the afterlife. I miss them and nothing feels adequate to fill that void. Yet I ask that You embrace me in Your compassionate arms and all who lament the loss of family and loved ones. May the tragedy of the cross remind me that there is still hope in the resurrection. Where in life there is turmoil, grant us triumph in this life and the next. Where there is pain give us new passion in our hearts for You. Be with me in sorrow and May the Holy Spirit

Desiree McCray

inhabit my tears. May each tear I cry water my seeds of faith for a brighter and lighter tomorrow. May their fallen souls rest in peace and may I rest in the knowledge that You accompany me now as I grieve.

In Jesus' Name. Amen.

—A PRAYER FOR REJECTS—

God Who accepts me,

Thank You for creating me in your image. While acceptance from others can feel good, help me to remember that I can't be so

afraid of losing people that I lose myself. I know I am not called to please everyone. Everyone is not going to like me, help me to accept this reality. Comfort me in the knowledge that I am perfectly known and loved by You. Your word says "whosoever shall not receive you, nor hear your words, when you depart out of that house or city, *shake the dust off of your feet*" (Matthew 10:14). God I choose to shake it off when people reject me. For when people reject me they are also rejecting You. I accept rejection as divine redirection. I accept rejection as divine protection because what God has for me is for me. What You have for me will not pass me by. I allow you

Desiree McCray

to order my steps and guide me to people who will love, cherish, and accept me. Help me to go where I'm celebrated not just where I am tolerated.

In Jesus' Name. Amen.

—A PRAYER FOR TRANSFORMATION—

God of Transformation,

    You took water and made it into wine.

    I know like the water I am being called to be transformed into whatever You desire me to be.

    I realize that I may have allowed others to drown out Your voice about who I am.

    Today I realize that I am in the middle of a process and I invite You into this process.

    I am not yet what You have called me to be, yet I am becoming all that You say I am.

    I surrender now confident that You will make something beautiful out of me. I don't lean on my understanding and I let go of the results.

In my Becoming may I know that whatever my gifts are, they look good on me.

Help me to be unique and unapologetic about who You are calling me to be.

Help me to be bolder for You.

Help me become more honest, more loving, more gracious, and more holy like You.

May the favor of the Lord our God rest on us.

Establish the work of our hands for us indeed.

In Jesus' Name. Amen.

—A PRAYER FOR TRANSITION—

God Who never Changes,

You are the God who goes before me, walks beside me, and comes behind me. You are the God who remains the same as yesterday,

today and tomorrow (Hebrews 13:8). I thank You that You are a certain God even in uncertain times. Thank You for every new opportunity and door You have opened. Calm my nerves and ease my anxieties surrounding this season of transition. I repent for not trusting in Your plan for my life. I declare that I need Your help. I declare that I do not fear change but instead I embrace change. I embrace You for who You are— the author writing the story of my life. Allow me to be still when life is rushing around me. I remember that You have great plans to prosper me— not to harm me (Jeremiah 29:11). I hold on to Your promises and I trust that every plan that I commit to

Desiree McCray

You will prosper according to Your perfect will and plan for my life. You promised me that You would never leave me nor forsake me (Deuteronomy 31:6). Be with me during this transition and give me peace about the things outside of my control. Make this transition stress free. Remind me that I don't have to know every detail of the future. Help me with each step I take in the right direction. Equip me for every good work (2 Timothy 3:17).

Encourage me and help me be excited about this transition. In the Mighty Name of Jesus of Nazareth.

Amen.

—A PRAYER FOR COURAGE—

Emmanuel (God is with us)

Thank You for being the God that goes with me wherever my feet take me. Have You not commanded me? Be strong and courageous. I am not afraid; I will not be discouraged, for the Lord our God will be with me wherever I go. (Joshua 1:9). I admit that sometimes it's easier to be stuck than move forward in courage and faith. Give me the courage to keep fighting. For Thou have given me strength this very hour. I am waiting for You. For God has not given us a spirit of fear and timidity, but of power, love, and self-discipline (2 Timothy 1:7). I take heart for greater is God who is in me than he that is in the World. (1 John 4:4). Drive out my fears. Close every door I have opened through fear in Jesus' Name. There is no fear in love. But perfect love drives out fear (1 John 4:18). I take courage and am not discouraged. I am encouraged to do what I am led

Desiree McCray

by Thine Spirit to do. Let me Roar boldly as a lion. Let me glorify You when I act and speak courageously for You. Let Your will be done for my life.

In Jesus' Name. Amen.

—PRAYER FOR DOUBT—

God of Blessed Assurance,

Like Thomas sometimes I doubt You. Life, hardships, and situations have given me a reason to turn away from You. Yet there still lies a glimmer of faith in me that keeps me coming back to You. So, I ask, Jesus, let me put my fingers in your wounds.

Lord, Let me touch You to see if You are real.^1

If I could touch the hem of Your garment, I know I could be made whole.

Draw me close to You.

Remind me that You do not judge me when I doubt but You can handle each one of my questions.

I invite You to show up and show out in my life.

Break the power of doubt in my life that prevents me from seeing your heart and hand.

Help me to trust You even when I can't trace You.

Help me to trust Your character even when I can't see you in my circumstances.

Open my eyes to see Your great and mighty works.

Build in me a powerful testimony so when I'm done doubting,

I can faithfully be a witness to others who are doubting too.

In Jesus' Name. Amen.

—PRAYER FOR REVIVAL—

Ancient of Days,

Will You not revive us again, that Your people may rejoice in You (Psalm 85:6)? Will you not send a refreshing to these dried bones? Will You not breathe into us new life to worship You again? For You said: If my people who are called by My name humble themselves, and pray and seek My face and turn from their wicked ways, then I will hear from heaven and will forgive their sin and heal their land (2 Chronicles 7:14). O God Your people turn to You. We turn back to You right now and pray that you would send Your spirit to revive us, refresh us and restore us. There has been drought and weariness and we pray that Holy Ghost fire ignites those dry places as tinder. Send wonderful rains of refreshing to our spiritual deserts. May the True Living Water quench our thirst and by the power of the Holy Spirit may You grace us. Give us a new heart and a new spirit to replace our old way of being. Revive our spirits. Revive our souls. Revive our families. Revive our schools. Revive our communities. Revive the nations. We implore You to do only what You can—miracles, signs, and wonders are evidence of Your presence. Not by might but by Your spirit, have Your way in our lives.

In the Name of Jesus the Christ of Nazareth. Amen.

—A PRAYER FOR PURIFICATION—

Elyon (God Supreme)

We thank You for being the prime example of purity in a fallen and broken world. We are a people of unclean lips. We thank You for loving us anyhow. Thank You that nothing can separate us from Your great love. We confess that we have jeopardized our purity by what we have allowed into our eyes, ears, minds, and hearts. Purify our hearts as only You can. Your word says, "If we confess our sins, he is faithful and just to forgive us our sins and to cleanse us from all unrighteousness" (1 John 1:9). Cleanse us. Wash us. Send Your purifying waters to wash away anything that does not benefit us, uplift us, or help us. As we pass through holy water, we are reminded of the baptism with water and baptism of the spirit. May we carry with us a spirit of purity that inspires others to follow You down a virtuous path that leads to eternal life. Cleanse us through Your holy fire (Numbers

31:23). Refine us in the fire so that we can emerge better and brighter than before. In Jesus' Name. Amen.

—PRAYER FOR HEALING—

Jehovah Rapha (The Lord Who Heals)

You are the Great Physician. Thank You for being the ultimate healer who heals all my diseases. Thank You for a reasonable portion of health and strength. I declare that You are Jehovah Rapha, the God who heals me. I pray that You will ease my suffering. Draw close to me for I call to You for help and You heal me (Psalm 30:2). I confess my sins before You that I may be healed. In Jesus' Name, I close every demonic door to affliction that was opened. Restore me to mental, physical, and emotional health according to Your will. Heal the wounds of my heart. Heal me from my past. Mend my brokenness for You bind up the broken-hearted (Psalm 147:3). May Your grace and life-altering power flow through every cell, every organ, every blood vessel, every tissue, and every fiber of my being. You promised to give power to the weak and increase the strength of those without might. You promised that those who wait for You will renew their strength; they shall mount up with wings like eagles, they shall run and not be weary they shall walk and not faint (Isaiah 40:29,31). Jesus, I declare by Your wounds I am healed (1 Peter 2:24). Send out Your word that I may be restored.

In Jesus' Name. Amen.

—A PRAYER FOR FAITH—

Covenant Keeping God,

Lord, we adore You. We confess that it is hard to keep faith in the End Times. It's hard to believe sometimes when disappointments occur again and again. It's hard to believe that You are able because so many others have failed me. Even though I can't see You, I still can see glimpses of Your working.

Lord, I thank You that You are a healer, a keeper, a Way-maker, and a miracle-working God. I am reminded that "faith is confidence in what we hope for and assurance about what we do not see" and "without faith, it is impossible to please God because anyone who comes to him must believe that He exists and that He rewards those who earnestly seek Him" (Hebrews 11:1,6).

So, here I am seeking You. Some people think I'm crazy or don't understand why I believe in a God I can't see. But I don't care how I look. I am unashamed to worship You. I am unashamed to profess my faith even to the skeptics. Help me to walk by faith and not by sight. I know that all things are possible for those who believe (Mark 9:23). I believe Lord, but I ask You to help my unbelief.

I know that nothing is too hard for You. I know that faith is a gift that can move mountains. Increase my faith. Decrease my doubt. Help me to trust that You have a plan for me to prosper me and not to harm me (Jeremiah 29:11).

In Jesus' Name. Amen.

ABOUT THE AUTHOR

Desiree McCray, 26, also known as Minister Des is a young prophetic voice for this generation. McCray stands as an nonbinary, womanist preacher. Along with preaching, Des is a conference speaker, poet, painter, published author, and host of the podcast titled "PROPHETIC SISTA GIRL."

McCray graduated in 2018 from the University of Missouri located in Columbia, Missouri with a Bachelor of Arts in English—Creative Writing. An award-winning preacher, Minister Des is a 2021 graduate with a Master of Divinity from Princeton Theological Seminary in Princeton, New Jersey. Des McCray seeks to make the gospel real and relevant by providing spiritual affirmation, divine inspiration, and radical transformation through the word of God.

blog: desforpres.wordpress.com
Instagram: @blaccwhoaman
Youtube: Des 4 Pres

BOOKS BY THIS AUTHOR

Hope Among Other Foods available on Amazon

Hope is (n.) a feeling of expectation. Among (prep.) surrounded by. Other (adj.) is of a different or distinct quality. Foods (n.) are consumable materials containing essential nutrients to maintain life and growth. Hope Among Other Foods: a concoction of fat girl poetry by Desiree McCray has ranging topics of racial marginalization, body, image, natural hair, navigating relationships, and womanhood. Feeding the soul while echoing a black religious experience, these words form a grand anthem of self-love, self-recognition, and self-definition.

FORTHCOMING BOOKS

My Sisters Look like God: a womanist manifesto through poetry by Desiree McCray (2023)

My Tongue cut loose: sermons from my prophetic, womanist, and black liberationist imagination by Desiree McCray (2023)

Made in the USA
Monee, IL
01 May 2023